AF447625

Born into Fear

BORN INTO, Volume 1

David Ballinger

Published by Consider Curiosity, 2024.

While every precaution has been taken in the preparation of this book, the publisher assumes no responsibility for errors or omissions, or for damages resulting from the use of the information contained herein.

BORN INTO FEAR

First edition. June 12, 2024.

Copyright © 2024 David Ballinger.

ISBN: 979-8224001552

Written by David Ballinger.

Also by David Ballinger

BORN INTO
Born into Fear

Standalone
The Philosophy of the LostxRabbitt
The Philosophy of the LostxRabbitt and Brimstone and Bandit part 1

Watch for more at https://free-5092953.webadorsite.com/.

For the unheard...

Chapter 1 Awakening:

*My first memory is a blur of noise and pain. A growling voice, hot
fetid breath on my face, and massive fingers constricting my windpipe. I
dangled helplessly in the air, tiny legs kicking at nothing. "Answer me!"
the booming voice demanded, spraying saliva across my terrified face.
Without words to reference, I couldn't fathom what was happening to
me. I could only experience it, not knowing what it was or even who
I was at this early stage of my existence. "Answer me, you little shit!"
he bellowed again. With no frame of reference, I searched through the
scant few memories I had in my short life and imagined a fairy tale
giant—livid about his missing goose. That's as close to an explanation as I
could draw a parallel from. But how could I answer? I was just a toddler,*

still practically an infant, barely able to walk without assistance. Words were a mystery, not yet formed in my still-developing mind.

All I could manage were feeble grunts and squeaks as that immense hand squeezed tighter around my neck, cutting off the precious air I was only then realizing I required. I marveled at the dark spots creeping into the edges of my vision, transfixed by the shapes contorting and swirling in kaleidoscopic shades of gray. The thunderous voice grew farther away, fading under the rush of blood pounding in my ears. Oblivion tugged at me, pulling me into its dark and merciful embrace. Then, just as everything began to go black, the massive fingers went slack. I plunged what seemed an endless distance before slamming into the hardwood floor with a jarring thud. I wheezed and gasped, gulping down the precious life-giving oxygen. Fear and confusion consumed my thoughts as I lay there afraid to move, pondering with what little consciousness remained,

"

Why would the universe wake me into this enigmatic nightmare?" That was my awakening. My first awareness of self and of pain.

Welcome to existence!! Let's introduce the performers who will be at the center of your universe. Let's give a warm welcome to Terror!!! Universally known for his role in every atrocity and mass genocide ever committed. A favorite of every third world dictator and would-be tyrant who ever thought of planet-wide conquest or just cleansing their own little part of it. Terror promises to keep you engaged in fight or flight for the foreseeable future. Now let's put our hands together and give a neurotic welcome to Pain, a veteran in this supporting role, always keeping Terror at center stage. But wait, our next esteemed guest is the not-to-be-upstaged loiterer behind the curtain, you guessed it: it's Confusion, keeping you out of every loop and falling through every crack all the while making sure you're always walking on eggshells and sitting on the edge of your seat with dreadful anticipation. This all-star cast is brought to you by the man you will soon come to know as Daddy! An all-star cast of characters guaranteed to leave you bruised and battered, mentally scarred, and an emotional wreck that no one would listen too even if you did tell them the horrible truth. I've often wondered over the intervening decades what karmic debts I must have acquired in the short time after my birth and still yet before the awakening, that I should be born into such misery. Well, that's a question for another time.

Chapter 2: The Submarine Commander

Nobody would believe the pure insanity I was subjected to. It was as if I had been born into some sort of deranged, twisted reality, one that existed solely to torture my newly conscious and subsequently broken spirit.

My stepfather – the looming, perpetual source of that torture – was a 6-foot-4 giant of a man. A nuclear submarine commander no less, who spent the Cold War years playing out a perilous game of tag with Russian submarines under the mock battlefield of the Arctic's icy depths. His size wasn't even the most imposing thing about him; he carried himself with an arrogant smugness, daring anyone to challenge his alpha status.

Incredibly, despite our ghastly and supremely dysfunctional father and son routine performed exclusively on the macabre set that was our home, he was somehow able to maintain the carefully crafted image of normalcy. To the outside world, we were just your average run-of-the-mill American family getting along as any other. My mother turned a intentionally blind eye, as did the rest of our extended family. Even though they knew the truth, vile and malignant - undulating just beneath the surface. I quickly learned that upholding appearances took priority over my wellbeing.

On the nights my mother took her precious Keeshond dogs to show competitions, the mask would slip. As if on cue, the second she pulled out of the driveway, my stepfather would begin his sick ritual. He'd barge into my bedroom, white inspection glove in hand, snapping it audibly against his wrist.

"This is how the Navy does inspections, boy," he growled, unable to prevent a hint of sadistic glee from flickering across his harsh features.

Then, with painstaking deliberation, he'd run that glove along every surface, checking for even a microscopic speck of dust or dirt. Needless to say, he always found some. Maybe a faint film on the top edge of the door frame that my six-year-old arms couldn't possibly reach. Or a slight haziness on the dresser his hulking six-foot-four frame blotted out.

The ritualistic humiliation wouldn't stop there. If his scrutiny turned up any imperfections, real or imagined, the sadistic games would begin. Vicious kicks and violent shoves, sending my tiny body crashing into walls and furniture. But I was a quick study in those days, honing an acrobatic agility borne from sheer self-preservation. I learned to twist my body at the moment of impact, using the momentum to redirect the blows into slap-shots that made the collisions look more damaging than they were. The harsh cracks as I bounced off drywall were still excruciating, but at least I avoided the sickening crunch of shattered bone.

It was during those torture sessions that I first uncovered my knack for acrobatics – the desperate flailing that allowed me to somersault and tumble across rooms when the explosive force of a well-placed kick sent me airborne. At the time, it was merely a means of preventing serious injury. Only later would I realize it had sparked something...an inordinately natural poise and body mastery. An unnatural ability manifested by the abnormal savagery of my childhood that would eventually allow me to backflip, whirl, and contort with an ease that defied conventional physical limitations.

After these harrowing bouts of ritualized violence and choreographed aerial combat, I'd hear my mom's car pull into the driveway, signaling the end of another evening's cruelty and humiliation.

My stepfather would collect himself and rush down the stairs to meet her at the door, head hung low in feigned regret.

"I did it again," he'd mutter, unable to completely mask the satisfaction bleeding into his voice.

My mother's response was always neutral, resigned. "Oh no...Jan!.... Oh well, come on then," she'd say with sympathy. Not for me, but for that poor, sick man who was burdened with the desire to assert dominance over a child who had no comprehension of what dominance even meant, much less assert it over anyone.

I could hear their footsteps ascending the stairs, dread coiling in my gut. My mom would gently crack open my bedroom door, peeking her head in with Jan hovering behind her like a carnivorous shadow.

"David, your dad is really sorry about what he did and wants to know if you're mad at him," she'd say in that sickly saccharine tone.

My inner voice would scream, "Goddamn right I'm mad, you sadistic fuck!" But by this time, my vernacular was masterfully honed, tuned to the song of survival. All I could muster while choking back tears of fear and rage was, "I could never be mad at you, Dad."

I can still remember the way fear and confusion boiled inside me, quickly culminating into a blinding panic as I saw that glove coming. How could this be real? Was I truly the only one who understood how gruesomely fucked up this entire situation was? What broke a person so completely that this sort of deranged behavior seemed normal to them?

Chapter 3: The Betrayal

The memories of those soul-crushing years in Tennessee still haunt me to this day. A fleeting glimmer of hope had wormed its way into my young mind, only to be mercilessly crushed under the cruel machinations of the very people who were supposed to protect me.

It was midway through second grade when our class was shown an after-school special about child abuse. As the grainy film flickered across the pull-down screen, scenes of families not unlike my own played out in brutal detail. Parents screaming unforgivable things, unwitting children

cowering in fear or being struck viciously. It was like watching my own life through a funhouse mirror - a twisted yet watered-down reflection, but still one that captured the essence of my own still private hell.

When the lights came back up, our teacher, Mrs. Hendricks, cleared her throat. She explained in a somber and restrained voice, "If any of you children are being abused or knew someone who was, you should come to my desk while the rest of the class has nap time." That this would be our chance to speak up without fear of repercussions.

My heart pounded in my tiny chest as I absorbed those words. Could this be my way out? Someone was finally acknowledging that the terrors I experienced daily were abnormal...criminal even. So, with the naive courage that only an eight-year-old could muster, I decided to seize that slim opportunity.

Waiting for what felt like an eternity, I finally crept up to Mrs. Hendricks' desk as my classmates slumbered, their steady breaths filling the room. With an initial gulp of air, I recounted a few of the articulable incidents with my stepfather, favoring ambiguity over specifics. To my surprise, Mrs. Hendricks didn't react with shock or horror. Instead, her expression remained placid, even bored as I struggled to find the most relatable words to convey the urgency of not telling my... Then, before I could finish that most pertinent of words, she gestured with a dismissive finger, raised the departmental phone to her ear, and requested that my parents be summoned to the school from their home on base, and shooed me away from her desk to wait in the hallway. I sat there for what seemed like hours, playing out wildly optimistic scenarios in my head of what would happen next. Surely, the teachers and administrators would step in to rescue me, to strip away the depravity that had tarnished my childhood. They were authority figures, after all, put in place to shield the young and defenseless from harm.

How painfully naive I was.

When my parents arrived, it was my own mother who ushered me into the main office, not a teacher or counselor. The second she entered and saw the grim looks on the administrators' faces, her jaw tightened and her eyes took on a cold, flinty sheen I had learned to dread. In that moment, I knew I had made an irredeemable mistake. My chance had been squandered.

The conversation deteriorated rapidly after that. Between bouts of my mother vehemently denying any possibility of abuse and Mrs. Hendricks feebly attempting to press the issue, I got the unavoidable sense that I had been written off as an attention-seeking brat, lashing out with tall tales against his family.

Near the end, my mother made a show of pulling me aside, fixing me with a look that could blister paint. "You can stop this nonsense right now," she hissed in a heated whisper. "Just tell them you made it up for laughs, to get out of class for a while. We can make this whole messy business go away if you cooperate."

Trapped, I did the only thing my impotent eight-year-old self could do - I complied. Obediently, yet reluctantly I recanted my accusations to the adults in an obviously coerced manner, mumbling that it had just been a joke that went too far. Everywhere I looked, I saw relief washing over the grown-ups' faces, eager to be unburdened of the awkward nature that accompanied making tough decisions.

A mother, a recenabe or tee in a reand,
chilobidi with cold eyes,

Admimisstrators wthea witodid off
at tentition-seeking brat.

aovoilde ictoratemomiss gtid,

Ethnically ambigaises styel.

Moments later, whilst being whisked away to the family sedan - like a third world dictator escaping an attempt on his life, my hand enveloped by my mother's crushing grip, I realized...No one was coming to save me. There were no valiant authorities going to swoop in and put a stop to these atrocious acts that threatened to prematurely end my pathetic existence. From that point on, I was completely and utterly alone.

Chapter 4: Realization of futility

Virginia Beach should have been a chance at a fresh start, a new beginning after the harrowing events in Tennessee. A chance to put that betrayal behind me and hold onto a semblance of hope that things could maybe, just maybe, improve someday. But the darkness lingered, stalking me with every new duty station as my stepfather's esteemed naval career advanced.

By fourth grade, I had become acutely aware that my home life was vastly divorced from that of the other children I encountered.

While they, unaware of my reality, enjoyed the after-school hours playing games and enjoying the unburdened innocence of childhood, my own days were spent walking through an ever-evolving minefield of trauma-inducing scenarios for abuse, trying to anticipate and avoid setting off the next eruption of rage from my short-fused stepfather. The harsh words, unforgivable accusations, and violence had only worsened with time, leaving me feeling like a cornered animal constantly bracing for impact.

One spring afternoon, I overheard a few neighborhood parents chatting outside as I sat alone in our yard, absently pulling up tufts of grass. Their conversation meandered from gardening to school functions before settling on an unexpected topic - when their teenagers would finally be old enough to move out on their own.

"Just two more years until Bobby's eighteen and out of the house!" one laughed in a tone approaching giddy relief. "Then it's smooth sailing for a while."

Eighteen. That fateful, hallowed age when kids finally gained the legal right to escape their childhood homes and parents. The notion of simply being able to pack up and leave once you became a legal adult had never really crossed my mind before. But as the weight of that overheard conversation slowly sank in, it triggered a cold, harsh succession of realizations.

First - holy shit, there was a definitive end date to the torment I faced daily. An expiration date, if you will, when the abuse would be forced to stop whether my parents willed it or not. Turning eighteen meant finally having the power to walk away and sever ties with my stepfather forever.

Second...holy shit, that date was still a full decade away for me.

I'll never make it that far, a small voice whispered inside my psyche, it's hopeless.

That cynical resignation triggered a spiral of desperate calculations, trying to gauge if the human body and spirit were truly capable of enduring such sustained anguish for that many more years. Images of all the times I had already been choked unconscious against the wall, struck with strategic open-handed blows to prevent telltale bruises, or squeezed until I couldn't breathe by that merciless grip formed between his thumb and fingers flashed in quick succession.

My stepfather was sickeningly adept at doling out pain and humiliation without leaving any physical marks that could be traced back to his behavior. No incriminating evidence, nothing that could jeopardize the facade of his uniform-clad, respected image in polite company. Just a young son's fractured psyche and eroding grasp on anything resembling normalcy.

Gauging it all with the kind of pragmatic stoicism that could only come from a boy who had been robbed of his childhood, my young mind struggled to discern if I possessed the fortitude to withstand nearly twice as much more punishment before that door to freedom finally opened.

In the end, I could reach no satisfying conclusion. Part of me dared to nurture a tendril of optimism that I could find a way to persevere through sheer force of will, if only the cruelty didn't intensify beyond my breaking point. But the cold, jaundiced part of my psyche - hardened by years of seeing the worst of human depravity first-hand - saw only a foreshortened future growing more bleak with each passing day.

What's more, a strange, nascent sense of existential dread began creeping in; a feeling that reality itself was fundamentally skewed, crafted not just by the abuse itself but by the willful blindness of all those authorities who had failed me. My mind struggled to reconcile how nobody else seemed aware of or willing to stop the insanity unfolding in our home. The sensation of being trapped in an elaborately orchestrated sham, a "Truman Show" where everyone but me was complacently playing along, calcified into an unshakable certainty.

If the world was willing to be so egregiously dishonest, who was to say the rules and boundaries of existence were as they seemed? Why stop at questioning my family's assertions - perhaps every adult's words were a deception, or every institution a facade. Maybe, just maybe, the entirety of reality itself was artificial, sustained by unseen puppet masters or a cold, uncaring machine mind like the one depicted in that book I'd heard whispers about: The Matrix.

As the neighborhood moms broke into a new peal of raucous laughter at the thought of their empty nests, I zoned back into the present, haunted by the pit of dread and borderline solipsism that had taken root in my young mind. Their whoops of joy sounded hollow, almost taunting, to my ears. In that moment, turning eighteen and gaining freedom felt like a leprechaun's vision, always just scant inches beyond my reach, there to torment me alone.

Chapter 5: The Line Crossed

For years, the depravity remained confined within the walls of our home, a closely guarded secret from the outside world. My stepfather was too careful, too adept at treading that precarious line between punishment and full-blown assault when it came to me. Sure, there were close calls where I wondered if that night's beating might finally be the one that landed me in the emergency room, unable to conceal the evidence of his brutality. But he always reined it in just short of that point, keeping the visible marks where they could be hidden or easily explained away.

Whether through force of habit or some genetic-born paternal instinct, he had never lain a hand on my younger half-brother Aaron – his own flesh-and-blood son - or my half-sister Janice, whose questionable lineage vaguely mirrored that of my own. Aaron was the slightly spoiled and whiny child who was bound to make lifestyle choices that our Bible belt ancestors would rather stayed in the closet - a Polish child, with dimpled cheeks and towheaded hair perpetually messed up in a cacophony of turns blurring the line between afro and perm. Maybe that's what stayed my stepfather's hand where Aaron was concerned. Or maybe it was Aaron's very existence that acted as a proverbial release valve for his tanked-up rage, allowing him and his addiction to domination and fear to be satiated through me alone.

For whatever reason, that line remained uncrossed...until the night it wasn't.

I'll never know what finally caused that dam to burst – whether it was a fleeting loss of control or a premeditated decision made through that crackling insanity that lurked behind his eyes. All I'll ever have are the images, burnt into my memory in scorching stop-motion, of the looming silhouette of my stepfather storming into the living room where my half-brother and I were watching cartoons. The sudden explosive movement as he seized Aaron by the arm and swung him into the air, like a human kite tail buffeted by the spittle-laced screams raining down from those jowled cheeks.

In an instant, the dynamic shifted in a way that was nearly impossible to process. No longer was I the sole stress-relieving punching bag absorbing his mindless rage. This...this was something entirely different that transcended the horrors I had already survived. A new dimension of depravity rendered in the terrified shrieks of an innocent child and the glazed look of psychopathic dissociation in my stepfather's bulging eyes.

Perhaps it was that foreign sound of authentic fear and anguish in Aaron's cries that finally snapped the remaining strands of my mother's denial. There are some things you can't ignore no matter how hard you try, some lines that can never be uncrossed no matter how deeply you bury your head in the sand.

That night, for the first and only time, she took action. A call was placed, mumbled utterances exchanged with professional detachment on the other end of the line. Then, with a whiplash-inducing abruptness, the police cruisers descended on our idyllic family home in a surreal convergence of flashing lights and barked orders.

In the end, my stepfather didn't even resist as they slapped on the cuffs and shoved him into the back of the squad car, still seething and eyes bulging with apoplectic rage. Perhaps somewhere in that tar-pit he called a soul, he knew he had finally crossed the Rubicon.

His stint in lockup was a painfully brief stent – a formality, really, reserved only for someone with his record of service and heroism on the nuclear submarines. Paperwork was shuffled, favors were called in, and the entire incident was efficiently swept aside by the preening officials in his chain of command, always eager to avoid any controversy that could tarnish the reputation of their vaunted submarine force. A mere slap on the wrist in the form of a temporary suspension and official reprimand in his service record was the extent of his punishment.

But there were some things that stayed with him, marks that couldn't be erased with a few pencil signatures and backroom handshakes. When he was finally released and the bruises from his stint in the brig had faded, an ugly raised wound remained carved across his upper lip – a permanent reminder in the form of a snarl, left behind by the heavy hands of whoever had taken offense to his presence in their pod. Man, I'd like to thank that guy.

The sight of that crimson gash greeted me as he stalked through our front door in the wake of his meager sentence. No words needed to be exchanged; we both knew the unspeakable line had been crossed and everything going forward would be forever...altered. That thin, mocking smile was the first thing I saw as he brushed past me without a word and made a beeline for the living room where my mother and Aaron were waiting with looks of dreadful anticipation.

A fierce spark of hope nearly broke through my usual pall of fatalism as he gathered his son in his arms. Perhaps hitting actual rock bottom would finally jar him back to whatever semblance of halting, shattered sanity he still retained. Maybe seeing the bruises inflicted on his own progeny would wake him to the horrific damage he was capable of, guilt him into changing his ways for good.

That tiny glimmer was immediately extinguished as he cupped Aaron's tender cheek with the underside of that sneering, mutilated lip and hissed a single contemptible phrase: "This is what happens to babies who defy me."

So much for second chances.

Chapter 6: The Point of No Return

In the aftermath of the incident with Aaron, an uneasy truce settled over our household. Gone were the explosive outbursts and overt physicality - at least where my half-brother was concerned. My stepfather seemed to recognize, however fleetingly, that he had ventured one step too far across a line that couldn't be uncrossed.

For me, though, the torment raged on unabated.

Perhaps realizing that the fallout from attacking his own son would be far more severe, he redirected the brunt of his sustained mania back onto his usual prey. The random bursts of irrational rage, the demeaning psychological games, the sudden flare-ups of violence - they all persisted and even intensified, compressed into an unrelenting torrent now that he was solely focused on me once again.

On the surface, we maintained an eerie facade of normalcy when out in public or entertaining relatives. He would play the part of the doting stepfather, hoisting me onto his lap and jostling me around in twisted parodies of roughhousing or cherished family memories being forged. All the while, that puckered scar where his lip had been split twisted into a haunting sneer, as if he derived some sick satisfaction from the charade.

It was during one of these perverted acts that I truly stared into the abyss of my stepfather's psychosis and glimpsed the horror of what he was ultimately capable of. As I obediently clambered onto his lap and we commenced the routine of forced laughter and exaggerated playfulness, his thick hand clamped over my mouth and nose, sealing them shut.

At first, I didn't comprehend what was happening, my naive child-mind dismissing it as just another rough aspect of his ineffectual imitation of paternal bonding. But as the seconds ticked by, the involuntary panic began to set in. The muffled sound of my own harsh breaths reverberating through the flesh-cage cupped over my face. The burning need for oxygen rapidly overwhelming all else.

That's when it hit me. The realization that this was no momentary lapse, no unintentional roughhousing taken a step too far. He wasn't just playing anymore - he was trying to kill me. Here, right out in the open mere feet from where my mother dotingly prepped dinner, blissfully unaware of her husband's depravity taking its next inevitable step.

I struggled against the immense weight of his arm pinning me back against his bullish chest, but it was no use. Helplessness washed over me as the terrifying possibility loomed that these could be my final moments. Drained of options, I made one last desperate play, thrashing with every fiber of being to break that infernal seal keeping life-giving air from reaching my lungs.

Time seemed to suspend in viscous slow motion as that heroic effort finally paid off in a precious half-second where his grip faltered, just enough for me to twist my burning face towards the open and let out a panicked, wheezing scream. It was a sound forged from the deepest, most primordial well of sheer desperation - half-bestial bellow, half-plea for the life I could feel slipping away.

Instantly, my mother rushed in from the kitchen, eyes already warily scanning for signs of fresh conflict even before her brain could process what her senses were relaying. To her, I must have looked like a deranged animal trapped in the clutches of some horrific beast, shrieking and flailing for freedom.

"What's going on in here?" She didn't wait for an answer before rounding on my stepfather, brow furrowing with an accusation she didn't quite dare voice aloud. Some lingering self-preservation instinct stilled her tongue, even as the truth must have played out before her eyes in stark clarity.

My stepfather didn't miss a beat, smoothly shifting into the role of aggrieved parent toward his unruly stepchild. A Trojan horse in our own home, laying siege to our lives through sheer, gaslighting persistence.

"Just horsing around and got a little carried away," he replied with a sheepish chuckle, purposefully loosening his grip to allow me shallow gulps of air. "Think his bratty wiggling was messing with my grip. Didn't mean to scare you."

He sealed the deception by ruffling my hair in an exaggerated gesture of avuncularity, as if we had just been playing a game that got slightly out of hand. But his eyes...his eyes told the real story. Chips of anthracite glittering with the banked embers of hatred boring directly into whatever shriveled, atrophied lumps of empathy still clung on in my mother's soul. A silent, daring communication that brooked no disagreement: This is how things are going to be, and you will fall obediently in line.

And shamefully, despicably, she did just that, as she had countless times before. Retreating from the living room with a murmured non-committal reply, her final sentence on the matter a defeated, "Just...be more careful with him next time. You know how rambunctious boys can get."

Translation: you have my perpetual benefit of the doubt to cross any line, no matter how unspeakable, as long as I can still cling to my precious illusions.

We never spoke of that incident again, but we didn't have to. It hung like a festering miasma in every interaction moving forward, an unspoken acknowledgment of the depravity he was willing to indulge, and how utterly defenseless I was against whatever psychological fantasy he chose to act out upon me.

Something snapped irreparably in my psyche in the aftermath. Up until that point, some infinitesimal part of me had clung to the naive belief that he ultimately wouldn't go too far, that he harbored some inviolable line of restraint when it came to the value of my life. That delusion was well and truly shattered, replaced with a new existential understanding - he never placed any value on my life, period. I was little more than a prop to be manipulated however he saw fit, my continued existence subject to his every whim.

From that point on, I truly disassociated, living in a numb, quasi-fugue state as the only defense against the horrors constantly surrounding me. My childhood wasn't just denied, it was flensed from my soul in layers of accumulated psychic trauma. I became a hollow, haunted automaton wearing the tattered form of a little boy, internally resolving to do whatever it took to endure until my eventual deliverance. Because for me, there were no more lines left to be crossed. Only the all-encompassing certainty that I was well and truly alone.

Chapter 7: The Manifestation

The trip to visit my mother's family in Oklahoma should have been a respite, however brief, from the relentless nightmare unfolding in our household. A chance to temporarily escape the dark cloud of oppression and catch a fleeting glimpse of what a normal, loving family looked like. But of course, that wasn't to be. The demons trailed us every mile of that endless road trip, lurking with bated breath for the opportune moment to pounce.

Word had gotten back to my uncle Roger about the incident with Aaron, as well as murmurs of the other unspeakable things happening behind closed doors. Outraged, he decided to confront my stepfather - the protector rising up to defend his baby sister's honor, incensed that anyone would dare mistreat her or the children she had brought into this world.

It started with a hushed, intense confrontation in the dimly lit den after the rest of the family had turned in for the night. Terse exchanges gradually escalated into shouting, then shoving, as my uncle grew increasingly exasperated with my stepfather's deflections and denials. The altercation finally boiled over in a frenzy of grappling limbs and traded blows, spilling out onto the front porch and eventually into the driveway, with my uncle giving vain chase.

I'll never forget the image of my stepfather scrambling into the driver's seat of our family sedan, uncle Roger diving through the open window after him like a patriotic GI storming a machine gun nest on some distant battlefield. Misplaced valor flashed across his contorted features as his meaty hands gripped the collar of that crisp uniform, fully invested in the delusion that a stern talking-to and some frontier justice would somehow solve everything.R6

Of course, reality swiftly intervened in the form of that cruel, puckered sneer creasing my stepfather's face. With a deftness that belied his burly frame, he twisted free and launched a volley of crunching strikes with a bare elbow, not stopping until Roger finally slipped backwards through the window and collapsed in a semi-conscious heap on the driveway.

In the end, it took several of the grown men in the extended family to pry them apart and restore order. I'll never know what words were ultimately exchanged between my uncle and my stepfather, but their separate expressions told the story well enough. One was still defiant, convinced he had done the right thing to protect his family. The other...the other held the smug satisfaction of a reigning alpha having brutally re-established dominion over his domain, confident no mortal force could threaten his reign.

A few days later, the forced frivolity resumed and our trunks were reloaded with fresh mementos from the aborted visit. But an unmistakable pall now hung over every forced embrace and performative well-wishing, the first whispers of disillusionment creeping in. There would be no refuge found here, no shelter from the gathering storms.

Yet in one clairvoyant moment, a crystalline truth rang out amidst the din, one that would indelibly shape my impressions of the world from that point onward. It came from that quietest of quarters - an overheard conversation between my mother and her youngest sister as they reminisced on happier times.

The talk, colored by just enough wine to loosen long-guarded tongues, eventually turned to past loves and missed opportunities. Voice hushed with wistfulness, my mother recounted her courtship and shotgun marriage to my birth father, a smiling young soldier who had managed to briefly sweep her off her feet. His image materialized from the gossamer threads of her words, taking ethereal form in my mind's eye...and as it did, the full weight of realization came crashing down.

My eyes. My nose. The precise timbre of my voice and cadence of my movements. Quite literally every single physical and mannerism attribute I possessed...all had been directly inherited from this mystery man who had briefly touched my mother's life before exiting as swiftly as he arrived.

In that moment, in the most literal sense imaginable, I was the unshakable living embodiment of my mother's infidelity. A permanent stain of the passion she had once felt for an idealized man of action, now souring into bile towards the bitter realities of the consolation prize she had settled for instead. I was the reminder she could never escape of decisions past, unwittingly manifested in flesh.

I can still hear the bitter finality underlying my mother's words as she drunkenly concluded her reverie to her rapt sister: "He was my one true love, but it wasn't meant to be. Some things just aren't..." That's when her gaze fell upon me, as if noticing my presence for the first time, knifing through any childish innocence that may have still remained with a look of unadulterated contempt. "But I'll always love him for giving me the greatest gift - this handsome young man who looks so much like his father."

The rest of that conversation is lost to the ravages of time and trauma. But I'll never be able to purge the macabre significance of that moment - the realization that merely existing, occupying the same physical realm as my stepfather, was the true unforgivable sin I could never atone for. How he must have felt every time he was forced to lay eyes upon me, helpless ire washing over him to be bound for life to this perpetual reminder of the wife who never truly wanted him in the first place.

After that night, I saw my own physicality through new, distorted lenses of self-loathing and alienation. This body, this personality...they weren't really mine after all. Just mocking caricatures, Frankenstein's monster stitched from the fading memories of my mother's youthful indiscretion and my stepfather's impotent rage over her perceived infidelity. A warped, Oedipal curse rendered in flesh and bone that both my progenitors were trapped in for life, decaying reminders of decisions they could never take back or rewrite. How could I ever escape that hell when the sources of their torment were inseparable from my very being?

Illustrations

BORN IN TO FEAR
By David Ballinger

DAVID BALLINGER

DAVID BALLINGER

A mother, a reentbe or tee in a reand,
chilobldi with cold eyes,

Admmisstrators wtheu witodud off
at tentition-seeking brat.

aovoilde ictoratemomiss gtid,　　　Ethnically ambigaises styel.

Into the Shadows: volume 2 in the Born Into series.
Teaser:

BORN INTO THE SHADOW

Chapter 1

The fluorescent lights hummed overhead, casting a sickly glow across the dingy meeting room. Plastic chairs were haphazardly arranged in a circle, some occupied, others left empty and abandoned like forgotten soldiers on a battlefield.

In a corner, apart from the circle, sat LeRoy. His fingers drumming a soothing rhythm on the armrests, in sync with the cadence of his internally audible pulse. The air felt thick, viscous, each shallow breath like trying to inhale molasses. His skin prickled with a cold sweat as waves of nausea rolled through his gut.

"Just breathe. In through the nose, out through the mouth." The therapist's words echoed hollowly in his mind. Easy for her to say from her ivory tower of sequestered ignorance. She didn't have to live inside LeRoy's head, a swirling vortex of rage- an ominous reminder of the rage lying just beneath the surface threatening to break his illusions of control.

Scanning the faces around the circle, he tried to find an anchor, something or someone he could tether himself too. Thud saving his ever slipping grasp on reality. A heavy-set woman, her cheeks glistening with tears. "She looks like she would be a good anchor" he thought as he shook his head bringing him back from his momentary foray into the crude. She spoke in a quivering voice about her violent husband. Then his gaze turned to an elderly man with faded tattoos and a stoic look on his face. He stared vacantly, his eyes portals to some ancient legacy of pain.

To LeRoy's left, a young woman fidgeted incessantly, her legs twitching spasms of pent-up energy. LeRoy's held back his urge to lash out, to unleash the fury simmering within. It grew ever harder to resist with every passing second. He could almost feel the phantom grip of his father's hand on his throate the searing blossom of pain across his cheek as the backs of those gnarled knuckles connected with flesh.

Not again. He wasn't that scared kid anymore, helpless and alone. He was a grown man, strong, and in control. This mantra played on a loop, but each repetition felt more and more hollow.

"Leroy" The gentle prod of the therapist's voice sliced through his turbulent thoughts. "Would you like to share today?"

All eyes turned towards the corner, weights of expectant judgment pressing down on his shoulders. He opened his mouth, What could he possibly say that they would understand? How could he articulate the constant, simmering rage, the monster perpetually clawing at the inside of his skull, demanding to be fed with the anguish of the ones who had ruined him.

Deep breaths. Just breathe. But the air refused to fully inflate his lungs, coming in ragged gasps. Sweat beaded on his brow, his t-shirt damply clinging to his back. The walls seemed to be closing in, the room shrinking around him.

> ◈ *"I...I have to The fluorescent lights hummed overhead, casting a sickly glow across the dingy meeting room. Plastic chairs were haphazardly arranged in a circle, some occupied, others left empty and abandoned like forgotten soldiers on a battlefield.*

In a corner, apart from the circle, sat LeRoy. His fingers drumming a soothing rhythm on the armrests, in sync with the cadence of his internally audible pulse. The air felt thick, viscous, each shallow breath like trying to inhale molasses. His skin prickled with a cold sweat as waves of nausea rolled through his gut.

"Just breathe. In through the nose, out through the mouth." The therapist's words echoed hollowly in his mind. Easy for her to say from her ivory tower of sequestered ignorance. She didn't have to live inside LeRoy's head, a swirling vortex of rage- an ominous reminder of the rage lying just beneath the surface threatening to break his illusions of control.

Scanning the faces around the circle, he tried to find an anchor, something or someone he could tether himself too. Thud saving his ever slipping grasp on reality. A heavy-set woman, her cheeks glistening with tears. "She looks like she would be a good anchor" he thought as he shook his head bringing him back from his momentary foray into the crude. She spoke in a quivering voice about her violent husband. Then his gaze turned to an elderly man with faded tattoos and a stoic look on his face. He stared vacantly, his eyes portals to some ancient legacy of pain.

To LeRoy's left, a young woman fidgeted incessantly, her legs twitching spasms of pent-up energy. LeRoy's held back his urge to lash out, to unleash the fury simmering within. It grew ever harder to resist with every passing second. He could almost feel the phantom grip of his father's hand on his throate the searing blossom of pain across his cheek as the backs of those gnarled knuckles connected with flesh.

Not again. He wasn't that scared kid anymore, helpless and alone. He was a grown man, strong, and in control. This mantra played on a loop, but each repetition felt more and more hollow.

"Leroy" The gentle prod of the therapist's voice sliced through his turbulent thoughts. "Would you like to share today?"

All eyes turned towards the corner, weights of expectant judgment pressing down on his shoulders. He opened his mouth, What could he possibly say that they would understand? How could he articulate the constant, simmering rage, the monster perpetually clawing at the inside of his skull, demanding to be fed with the anguish of the ones who had ruined him.

Deep breaths. Just breathe. But the air refused to fully inflate his lungs, coming in ragged gasps. Sweat beaded on his brow, his t-shirt damply clinging to his back. The walls seemed to be closing in, the room shrinking around him.

"I...I have to..."

Don't miss out!

Visit the website below and you can sign up to receive emails whenever David Ballinger publishes a new book. There's no charge and no obligation.

https://books2read.com/r/B-A-QGDKB-VLCLD

BOOKS2READ

Connecting independent readers to independent writers.

About the Author

My story isn't mine it's the story of millions that came before me. I happen to be blessed enough for my memory and my mind to be intact enough so I could put words to paper to get our story out in the public consciousness.

Read more at https://free-5092953.webadorsite.com/.

www.ingramcontent.com/pod-product-compliance
Lightning Source LLC
Chambersburg PA
CBHW051317160726
47994CB00003B/1504